855
WAYS TO
SAY
SAID

A "Writing By Midnight" Resource

By: Midnight Taylor

ISBN 978-1-329-03827-1

Published By:
Midnight & Co.
Punta Gorda, Fl 33950
midnight@midnighttaylor.com

More from Midnight Taylor at
www.midnighttaylor.com

Follow Midnight on Facebook
www.facebook.com/midnightleitaylor

Follow Midnight on Twitter
www.twitter.com/midnight_taylor

Join Midnight's Writing Group
https://www.facebook.com/pages/Writing-By-Midnight/707914732656268

Join Midnight's Newsletter
http://midnighttaylor.com/newsletter/

Don't miss out on my FREE e-report
6 Secrets of Successful Writers!
Available at:
www.midnighttaylor.com/free-writing-guide

Table of Contents

Expand and Improve Your Vocabulary – WHY?

Many people associate expanding vocabulary with writers, speakers and people with higher education; when, in reality, everyone should strive to expand their vocabulary every single day. Boosting the number of words you understand and have at your disposal should be a lifelong pursuit. Why should you make this a goal of yours? Simple, a large vocabulary gives you the ability to say what you mean.

Remove Empty Words
Have you ever had someone say "I'm sorry" so many times that it just loses its meaning? Or where everything was "awesome," and the only distinction was "really awesome" and "kinda awesome?" If a person has a limited vocabulary they are forced to use the same words repeatedly and this overuse removes the meaning. It gets tiring and it's difficult to know what they mean. Sure, they're giving you a word or phrase but do you know what they **mean**? These words take the form of verbiage but don't offer any substance. That's why I call them "empty words," which can be compared to empty calories. They look and sound like words but they offer no substance; this leaves your listeners and readers hungry and wanting more, feeling unsatisfied.

Think of your vocabulary as your toolbox. You don't use just a chainsaw to create a sculpture. You would need a set of tools designed for that specific job. Adding to your toolset (vocabulary) allows you to make finer distinctions in what you mean and gives you the opportunity to be explicit in what you're saying instead of a general vagueness. When you bolster your vocabulary and add more and more tools this will allow you to say what you mean and remove empty words and worse empty intensifiers, which are also called adverbs. Examples of empty intensifiers are really, very, and quite. Just leave those in the bottom of the box.

Understand More

I would take a guess and say that there is a large portion of the populace that when they come across a word they are unfamiliar with, either in reading or listening, they just skip over it. When someone does this, they lose part of the message. When a person ignores a word they don't understand, they miss the entire meaning that was being presented to them. The meaning may have been a thought, an emotion, an idea, or something very important. If a person misses out on enough words . . . the effect can be very detrimental.

It's very beneficial to have a diverse vocabulary. You'll be able to understand what you read and receive the message in full. That's all communication is - the giving and receiving of messages. The way we interpret those messages is fundamental in our communication with each other and the world. Much like learning a language that is foreign to you, giving yourself a wide range of options in your own language can open many doors for you. It drastically improves your ability to grasp and understand ideas; which, allows you to think more logically and incisively. Also, the more you understand the more informed and involved citizen you can be. Instead of repeating yourself multiple time with the same range of words and getting frustrated that the conversation is going in circles and you're not getting your point across, you can instead, focus and give more precise meaning to your message.

Communicate To Others

When you have a masterful command of words and language you will naturally have more powerful and engaging speech and writing. Several studies over the years have shown a direct correlation between a person's vocabulary and their success. The larger the person's vocabulary, the more likely they are to be successful in their endeavors. Let's take a look at why this might be.

Just as it makes it easier for you to understand other people, having a larger vocabulary makes it easier for them to understand you. With a diverse vocabulary you can communicate effectively with a wide range of people. Having this ability doesn't limit your options, as a smaller vocabulary would. In today's society, it's difficult for some to believe that they should be judged by the way they speak. However unbelievable it may seem, it is inevitably true. The way you articulate yourself often reflects your level of education. The level of education you achieve is often linked to what and how much you understand. People who have a greater level of understanding and knowledge are able to go further in their professional lives. Professional success depends on thinking and communication skills. It's true that if you know about your area of expertise well enough the level of education may not be necessary, however, if you don't have the skills and ability to **communicate** the knowledge that you do have, you're not going anywhere.

"The difference between the right word and the almost right word is like the difference between lightning and a lightning bug." ~Mark Twain~

Attain and Retain Attention
As I stated before, the use of repetitive words from a limited vocabulary can become boring and uninteresting for your listeners and readers. Their eyes will glaze over and they will move on. When you have prolific vocabulary you can grab their attention and more importantly keep it. This is the key for great leaders; they must gain the interest of the people and then retain it long enough to gain their allegiance. When a person is able to articulate themselves well they are able to express themselves confidently. They are not repeating themselves and they don't have to take time to find the right word. They are able to use the right word, at the right time. When this ability is present, it makes a good impression, and we all know what they say about first impressions. Also, with this level of confidence exhibited, the level of self-esteem is also on par with it.

Did you know that Malcom X only achieved eight years of education? He spent his time in jail copying pages from a dictionary to improve his vocabulary. When he was released, he had achieved his goal and had the ability to speak to, persuade and inspire many people.

Why Improve Vocabulary?

It's not necessary to consume an entire dictionary to enrich your life with a rich vocabulary. Just gradually learning a few words a day will increase your knowledge of language significantly. Most people try to improve themselves and their lives and the lives of the ones they love. Your ability to express yourself well is no different. When you expand yourself in this way it opens your mind to new ideas and opportunities. You'll be able to understand so much more and when you can communicate your thoughts effectively, it gets the results you want.

There is a reason that man created speech, writing, language and words. The cave-man grunts and moans don't get you very far and often don't end the way you'd like. Give yourself the ability to choose your words with greater precision. Sharpen your communication. Gain a masterful command of words. Get rid of empty words and empty intensifiers. Give into this lifelong pursuit. Improve your confidence. Raise your self-esteem. Enhance your life.

Purpose

The purpose of this book is to provide an inclusive list of synonyms of "said," for all those that wish to expand and improve their vocabulary. This book is not just for writers, teachers and students. It is also for the common man that just wishes to add a valuable resource to their life.

This is a great resource for teachers and students. There is not a more comprehensive list available online, except perhaps an actual dictionary. Give your classroom and students an extra boost with their learning and vocabulary.

There are 855 ways to say said listed here and I have included their corresponding definitions. This is much more useful than a meaningless list of words. With this list you can be sure to find, learn and utilize the precise word that articulates the meaning you want to express. I hope that it is helpful to you.

In any case I would appreciate if you left a review. Whether you find this a valuable resource or waste of time, I want to hear about it. Please find this book on Amazon and leave a review or send me an email at midnight@midnighttaylor.com

abjured	to renounce or retract, especially with formal solemnity
accused	to charge with the fault; to find fault with
acknowledged	to admit to be real or true; to show or express recognition of realization of
acquiesced	to assent tacitly; submit or comply without protest
acquired	to gain for oneself
added	to unite or join to increase the number, quantity, size or importance
addressed	to direct a speech to; to use a specified form or title in speaking
adjured	to charge, bind or command earnestly and solemnly; to entreat or request earnestly or solemnly
admitted	to confess or acknowledge; to concede; to permit the possibility of something
admonished	to caution, advise or counsel against something; to reprove or scold
adumbrated	to produce a faint image or resemblance of; to foreshadow
advanced	to bring into consideration; suggest

advertised	to announce or praise in some public medium; to give information to the public about
advised	to give counsel to; to recommend as desirable, wise, prudent
advocated	to speak in favor of; support or urge by argument; recommend publicly
affirmed	to state or assert positively; to confirm or ratify
agonized	to put forth great effort of any kind; suffered extreme pain or anguish
agreed	to have the same views, emotions; to give consent
alerted	to warn
alleged	to assert without proof; to declare with positiveness
allowed	to give permission to or for; to let have
alluded	to refer casually or indirectly
allured	to attract or tempt by something flattering or desirable
amazed	to fill with incredulity or surprise
angled	to turn sharply in a different direction; to attempt to get something by sly or artful means
animadverted	to comment unfavorably or critically
announced	to make known publicly or officially; to state the approach or presence of
answered	to speak in response
apologized	to offer an apology or excuse for some fault; to make a formal defense in speech
appealed	to ask for aid, support, mercy, sympathy or the like

appeased	to bring to a state of peace, quiet, ease, calm or contentment; pacify; to satisfy
approved	to speak favorably of; to consent or agree to
argued	to present reasons for or against; to dispute
articulated	to utter clearly and distinctly; pronounce with clarity
ascertained	to find out definitely; to learn with certainty
asked	to make inquiry; to request
assented	to agree or concur; to give in
asserted	to state with assurance, confidence or force; state strongly
assessed	to judge the worth, importance; evaluate
asseverated	to declare earnestly or solemnly; affirm positively
assumed	to take for granted or without proof; to take upon oneself
assured	to declare earnestly to; inform or tell positively
astonished	to fill with sudden and overpowering surprise or wonder
attacked	to set upon in a forceful, violent, hostile or aggressive way
attempted	to make an effort at; try
attested	to bear witness to; certify
attributed	to regard as belonging to, produced by or resulting from
augured	to divine or predict; to conjecture from signs or omens
authorized	to give authority or official power to; formally sanction; empower

averted	to turn away or aside; to ward off; prevent
avoided	to keep away from; keep clear of; to prevent from happening
avouched	to make frank acknowledgment or affirmation of; declare or assert with positiveness; to assume responsibility for; guarantee
avowed	to declare frankly or openly; own; acknowledge
awakened	to awake; to spring into being, arise, originate
awed	to inspire with awe

babbled	to utter sounds or words imperfectly, indistinctly; to talk idly, irrationally or excessively
backed	to provide support
backpedaled	to retreat from or revers one's previous stand on a matter
back talked	to answer back
badgered	to harass or urge persistently
baited	to entice by deception or trickery so as to entrap or destroy
bantered	to exchange light, playful, teasing remarks
bargained	to discuss the terms of; to come to an agreement
barked	to utter in a harsh shouting tone
barreled	to move very fast
bawled	to cry or wail lustily
beamed	to emit or smile radiantly or happily
beckoned	to signal, summon or direct; to lure
began	to proceed to perform the first or earliest part
begged	to ask for as a gift, as charity or as a favor; to ask to give or do something
beguiled	to influence by trickery, flattery

believed	to have confidence in the truth, the existence or the reliability of something
belittled	to regard or portray as less impressive or important than appearances indicate; depreciate
bellowed	to emit a hollow, loud, animal cry; to roar; to utter in a loud deep voice
belted out	to carry a tune; to loudly emit noise
bemoaned	to express distress or grief over; to regard with regret or disapproval
berated	to scold; rebuke
beseeched	to implore urgently; to beg eagerly for
besought	to implore urgently; to beg eagerly for
bespoke	to ask for in advance
bestowed	to present with ;give; confer
betrayed	to deliver or expose by treachery or disloyalty
bid	to command; order; to express
bit into	to cut into sharply or harshly
blabbed	to reveal indiscreetly and thoughtlessly; to talk or chatter thoughtlessly
blamed	to hold responsible; find fault with
blasted	to produce a loud, blaring sound
bleated	to give forth with or as if with a bleat; to utter a sound resembling the cry of a sheep, goat or calf
blew up	to overwhelm with emotion; to violently express
blubbered	to weep noisily and without restraint; to say incoherently while weeping
blurted	to utter suddenly or inadvertently; divulge impulsively

blustered	to roar; to be loud, noisy or swaggering; utter loud, empty menaces or protests
boasted	to speak with exaggeration and excessive pride
boded	to announce beforehand; predict; to be an omen of
boomed	to make give forth with a booming sound; to make a deep prolonged resonant sound
bragged	to speak with exaggeration and excessive pride
breathed	to control the outgoing breath in producing voice and speech sounds
broached	to mention or suggest for the first time
broadcasted	to make something known widely
broke in	to interrupt; to insert into conversation
brought forth	to bring about
brown-nosed	to curry favor
bruited	to voice abroad; rumor
buckled	to prepare oneself to apply oneself; to give into
bullied	to be loudly arrogant and overbearing
butted in	to project into conversation; to interrupt
buzzed	to speak or murmur with a low, vibrating, humming sound

cackled	to laugh in a shrill, broken manner; to utter with a shrill, broken sound or cry
cajoled	to persuade by flattery or promises
calculated	to determine by reasoning, common sense or practical experience; estimate
called	to cry out in a loud voice; shout
called for	to command or request to come; summon
called on	to bring attention to or summon on
came clean	to tell the truth
cannonaded	to attack continuously with or as if with cannon
caroled	to praise or sing, in a lively, joyous manner
carped	to find fault or complain querulously or unreasonably
categorized	to describe by labeling or giving a name to
caterwauled	to utter long wailing cries
cautioned	to give warning to
censored	to delete parts that include the manner or morality
censured	to criticize or reproach in a harsh or vehement manner

chaffed	to mock, tease or jest in a good-natured way
challenged	to call in question; to summon to a contest of skill, strength, etc.
championed	to defend or support
changed	to alter or modify
chanted	to sing or utter in a short simple melody in which several words are assigned to one note
charged	to attribute to
chastised	to criticize severely
chatted	to converse in a familiar or informal manner
chattered	to talk rapidly in a foolish or purposeless way
cheated	to deceive
cheeped	to chirp; to utter characteristic shrill sounds
cheered	to salute with shouts of approval, congratulation, triumph; to gladden or cause joy to
chided	to express disapproval of; to harass
chimed	to sound harmoniously
chipped in	to interrupt a conversation; to contribute
chirped	to make a characteristic short, sharp sound
choked	to become or cause to become speechless; to have stuttered speech from the effect of emotion or stress
chortled	to express with a gleeful chuckle
chuckled	to laugh to oneself
churned	to agitate; to turn over

cited	to quote; to mention in support, proof or confirmation
claimed	to demand by or as by virtue of a right; to assert and demand the recognition of
clamored	to raise an outcry; to utter noisily
clarified	to make clear or intelligible
clucked	to make a clucking sound; express concern, approval, etc.
coaxed	to attempt to influence by gentle persuasion, flatter
comforted	to sooth, console, or reassure
commanded	to direct with specific authority or prerogative
commentated	to deliver or make explanatory or critical comments
commented	to make remarks, observations or criticisms
communed with	to mutually exchange information; to communicate with
communicated	to impart knowledge of; to give or interchange thoughts
complained	to express dissatisfaction, pain, uneasiness, resentment or grief
complimented	to express praise, commendation or admiration
conceded	to acknowledge as true, just or proper; to make concession; yield
conceited	to flatter; to be vain, proud, or egotistical
concluded	to bring to an end; to say in conclusion
concurred	to accord in opinion; to cooperate
condemned	to express an unfavorable or adverse judgment on

condescended	to behave patronizingly
conferred	to consult together
confessed	to acknowledge or avow; to own or admit as true
confided	to impart secrets trustfully; to discuss private matter or problems
confirmed	to establish the truth, accuracy, validity or genuineness of
confused	to make unclear or indistinct
confuted	to prove to be false, invalid or defective
congratulated	to express pleasure to; to express sympathetic joy or satisfaction
conjectured	to conclude or suppose from grounds or evidence insufficient to ensure reliability
consented	to agree to; to comply or yield
considered	to regard as or deem to be; to think carefully about
consoled	to alleviate or lessen the grief, sorrow or disappointment of; give solace or comfort
conspired	to act or work together secretly; to plot
construed	to give the meaning or intention of; to deduce by inference or interpretation
consulted	to seek advice or information from; to refer to for information
contained	to hold or include within
contended	to struggle in opposition
contested	to struggle for victory or superiority
continued	to go on after suspension or interruption; to go on

contradicted	to assert the contrary or opposite of; to deny directly
contributed	to give or furnish with
controlled	to exercise restraint or direction over; to hold in check
conveyed	to communicate; to transmit or transfer
convicted	to prove or declare guilty;
convoluted	to twist, or complicate
convulsed	to shake violently; agitate; to cause to shake violently with laughter, anger, pain
cooed	to murmur or talk fondly or amorously
corrected	to set or make true, accurate or right; to point out errors
corroborated	to make more certain
cosigned	to join
coughed	to expel by coughing; to expel air from the lungs suddenly with a harsh noise
counseled	to give advice to
countered	to meet or answer by another in return
crabbed	to say in a grouch, ill-natured or irritable manner
cracked	to break with a sudden, sharp sound
craved	to long for, want greatly
credited	to put confidence in; to ascribe to
cried	to utter inarticulate sounds, especially of lamentation, grief or suffering
criticized	to censure or find fault with; to judge or discuss the merits and faults of

croaked	to speak with a low, rasping voice
crooned	to sing in an evenly modulated, slightly exaggerated manner
cross-examined	to examine by questions intended to check a previous examination
crossed	to put across; to move, pass or extend
crowed	to utter an inarticulate cry of pleasure; to gloat, boast or exult
cued	to provide with a cue or indication; prompt
cursed	to wish or invoke evil; to swear
cussed	to use profanity

D

debated	to engage in argument or discussion
deceived	to mislead by a false appearance or statement
decided	to solve or conclude; to determine or settle
deciphered	to make out or discover the meaning of
declaimed	to speak aloud in an oratorical manner
declared	to make known or state clearly; to announce officially
declined	to withhold or deny consent
decoded	to extract meaning from
decreed	a formal and authoritative order
defended	to ward off; to maintain by argument, evidence; uphold
deflected	to turn from a true course; to turn aside
delivered	to give to another
deluded	to mislead the mind or judgment
demanded	to ask for with proper authority
demurred	to make objection
denied	to state that something is not true; to refuse to agree to

denoted	to mark or signal
denounced	to condemn or censure openly; to make a formal accusation against
depicted	to represent by; portray; describe
deplored	to regret deeply; to disapprove of
depreciated	to lessen the value of
derided	to laugh at in scorn or contempt
described	to tell or depict; to give an account of; to pronounce as or label
designated	to mark or point out
detailed	to relate or report with complete particulars
detected	to discover or catch
determined	to settle or decide; to conclude or ascertain
developed	to bring out the capabilities or possibilities of; to cause to grow or expand
dictated	to say or read aloud; to prescribe or lay down authoritatively
digressed	to deviate or wander away from the main topic
directed	to manage or guide by advice; to regulate the course of
disagreed	to differ in opinion; to fail to agree
disapproved	to withhold approval from; to decline; to think wrong or reprehensible
disavowed	to disclaim knowledge of, connection with or responsibility for
disclaimed	to deny or repudiate interest in or connection with
disclosed	to make known; reveal or uncover

discovered	to notice or realize
discussed	to consider or examine by argument, comment
dismissed	to bid or allow to go
disparaged	to speak of or treat slightly
disproved	to prove to be false or wrong
disputed	to engage in argument; to argue vehemently
disrupted	to cause disorder or turmoil; to destroy the normal continuance; interrupt
disseminated	to scatter or spread widely
divulged	to disclose or reveal
dodged	to elude or evade by a sudden shift of position or by strategy
drafted	to outline or plan; compose
drawled	to say or speak in a slow manner
dredged up	to unearth or bring notice to; to locate and reveal by painstaking investigation or search
droned	to speak in a monotonous tone

eased	to abate in severity; reduce awkwardness
echoed	to repeat or imitate
edited	to check and improve accuracy
ejaculated	to utter suddenly and briefly; exclaim
elaborated	to add details to; to work out carefully
elucidated	to make lucid or clear; explain
eluded	to avoid or escape; to escape the understanding, perception or appreciation of
embellished	to enhance with fictitious additions
emitted	to send forth; to give forth
empathized	to experience or engage in the intellectual identification with or vicarious experiencing of the feelings, thoughts, or attitudes of another
emphasized	to lay stress upon
encouraged	to inspire with courage, spirit or confidence; to stimulate by assistance, approval
ended	to bring to a conclusion; to terminate
endowed	to provide with
enjoined	to prescribe with authority or emphasis; to direct or order to do something

enjoyed	to experience with satisfaction, joy or pleasure
enounced	to utter or pronounce; to announce declare or proclaim
enticed	to lead on by inciting hope or desire
entreated	to ask earnestly
enumerated	to mention separately; specify, as in a list; to ascertain the number of
enunciated	to utter or pronounce in an articulate manner; to state or declare definitely
equivocated	to use ambiguous or unclear expressions
escalated	to raise or lower; to increase in intensity
estimated	to form an opinion of; to form an approximate judgment or opinion
eulogized	to praise highly
evaded	to escape from by trickery or cleverness
evinced	to show clearly; to reveal the possession of; make evident
exaggerated	to magnify beyond the limits of truth; to represent disproportionately
examined	to inspect or scrutinize carefully
exclaimed	to cry out or speak suddenly and vehemently, as in surprise, strong emotion, or protest
excused	to regard or judge with forgiveness or indulgence; to give pardon or forgiveness
exhibited	to offer or expose to view; present for inspection; to manifest or display
exhorted	to urge, advise or caution earnestly
expatiated	to enlarge in discourse or writing; be copious in description or discussion

expected	to look forward to; regard as likely to happen; anticipate the occurrence of
expiated	to atone for; make amends
explained	to make plain or clear; to make known in detail
explicated	to make plain or clear; to develop
exploded	to suddenly and violently burst
exposed	to lay open to something specified; to lay open to danger
expostulated	to reason earnestly with someone against something that person intends to do or has done
expounded	to set forth or state in detail; to explain
expressed	to put into words; to show or reveal
extended	to stretch out; to reach out
extolled	to praise highly

falsified	to make false or incorrect
faltered	to speak hesitatingly or brokenly
fantasized	to conceive fanciful or extravagant notions or ideas
favored	to prefer; treat with partiality
feared	to be afraid of; to have reverential awe of
feigned	to represent fictitiously; to make believe; to pretend
fessed up	to admit or concede
fibbed	to tell a lie
figured	to compute or calculate
finished	to bring to an end or to completion
fired off	to begin to talk and continue without slackening
fired back	to reply quickly
fished	to search carefully; to catch or attempt to catch
flabbergasted	to overcome with surprise and bewilderment
flirted	to court triflingly or act amorously without serious intentions; playfully
floundered	to struggle clumsily or helplessly

foreshadowed	to show or indicate beforehand
foretold	to tell of beforehand
forewarned	to warn in advance
formulated	to express in precise form; state definitely; to devise or develop
founded	to establish on a firm basis
framed	to form, devise or compose; to incriminate an innocent person with false evidence
fretted	to express worry, annoyance or discontent; to torment, irritate or annoy
frowned	to express displeasure or deep thought
fumed	to be overcome with anger or fury
fussed	to make much ado about trifles; to complain; to disturb

gabbed	to talk or chat idly
gagged	to stop up the mouth; to choke
gasped	to catch one's breath; to struggle for breath; to utter with gasps
gave	to present voluntarily
gawped	to stare with the mouth open in wonder or astonishment
gibbered	to speak inarticulately or meaninglessly; to speak foolishly
giggled	to laugh in a silly high-pitched way
gloated	to look at or think about with great or excessive, often smug or malicious, satisfaction
gloomed	to look sad, dismal or dejected; to fill with gloom
glossed	to give a false or deceptively good appearance to
glowered	to look or stare with sullen dislike, discontent or anger
goaded	to push at or drive at; incite
gossiped	to talk idly
granted	to bestow or confer
grated	to have an irritating or unpleasant effect

greeted	to address with some form of salutation; to meet or receive
grimaced	to contort the face
grinned	to smile broadly
griped	to complain naggingly or constantly
groaned	to utter a deep, mournful sound expressive of pain or grief
groveled	to humble oneself or act in an abject manner, as if in great fear or utter servility
growled	to utter a deep guttural sound of anger or hostility; to murmur or complain angrily
grumbled	to murmur or mutter in discontent; to utter low, indistinct sounds
grunted	to utter a deep guttural sound
guaranteed	to make oneself answerable for something; to secure
guessed	to estimate or conjecture about correctly
guffawed	to laugh loudly and boisterously
gulped	to swallow rapidly
gurgled	to flow in a broken, irregular way
gushed	to flow out or issue suddenly; to express oneself extravagantly or emotionally

haggled	to bargain in a petty, quibbling and often contentious manner
harped	to dwell on persistently or tediously
hastened	to hurry or caused to hurry
hastened to add	to be anxious to add to the conversation
hastened to say	to be anxious to say something
heckled	to harass with impertinent questions or gibes
hedged	to avoid a rigid commitment; evade; stall
heeded	to give careful attention to
held	to remain fast; to hold back
hemmed and hawed	to discuss, deliberate or contemplate rather than taking action; to mumble and procrastinate in one's speech
heralded	to give news or tidings of; to indicate or signal the coming of
hesitated	to be reluctant or wait to act
hinted	to make indirect suggestion or allusion
hissed	to express disapproval of by hissing
hollered	to cry aloud, shout or yell

hooted	to cry out or shout
horned in	to intrude into conversation; to interrupt
howled	to utter a loud, prolonged, mournful cry
huffed	to treat with arrogance or contempt
hurled	to throw or fling with great force or vigor
hypothesized	to form or assume a theory

I

incited	to stir, encourage, or urge on
identified	to recognize or establish as being a particular person or thing
idled	to spend or waste time; to run slowly
illustrated	to clarify one's words with examples and details
imitated	to mimic
imparted	to make known; to give
implied	to indicate or suggest without being explicitly stated
implored	to beg urgently or piteously
imported	to bring in or introduce
indicated	to point out; direct attention to
indulged	to yield to an inclination or desire
inferred	to derive by reasoning
informed	to five or impart knowledge of a fact or circumstance
initiated	to introduce into the knowledge of some subject
inquired	to seek information by questioning
inserted	to put or place in; to introduce; interject

insinuated	to suggest or hint slyly
insisted	to be emphatic, firm, or resolute on some matter of desire, demand or intention
instigated	to cause by incitement; to urge, provoke or incite
instructed	to furnish with knowledge; to furnish with orders or directions
insulted	to treat or speak to insolently or with contemptuous rudeness
interjected	to insert between other things
interposed	to place between; cause to intervene; to put between or in the way of
interpreted	to give or provide the meaning of
interrogated	to examine by questions
interrupted	to break or cause to cease
interviewed	to question, consult or evaluate another person
intimated	to indicate or make known indirectly
intimidated	to make timid; fill with fear
intonated	to utter with a particular tone or modulation of voice
intoned	to utter with a particular tone or voice modulation
introduced	to present to another
inveighed	to protest strongly or attack vehemently with words
inveigled	to entice, lure or ensnare by flatter or artful talk
investigated	to examine, study or inquire into systematically
invited	to request politely

invocated	to invoke
invoked	to call for with earnest desire; to call on
irrationalized	to make or cause to be irrational
irritated	to excite to impatience or anger; annoy
itemized	to list or state by items

jabbered	to talk or utter rapidly, indistinctly, incoherently, or nonsensically
jeered	to speak or shout derisively
jested	to speak in a playful, humorous or facetious way
joined in	to collaborate with or interject into
joked	to speak in a playful or merry way; to say something in a fun or teasing way
joshed	to chaff; banter in a teasing way
judged	to form an opinion or estimate
jumped in	to collaborate with or interject into
justified	to defend or uphold as warranted or well-grounded

keened	to wail in lamentation for the dead
kibitzed	to offer advice or critique as a spectator
kicked in	to collaborate with or interject into

laid out	to give an account or representation
lambasted	to reprimand or berate harshly
lamented	to express sorrow or regret
lashed out	to speak sharply
lauded	to praise
laughed	to express mirth, pleasure, derision or nervousness
lavished	to expend or give in great amounts or without limit
leaked	to allow to become known
lectured	to rebuke or reprimand at some length
leered	to look with a sideways or oblique glance
leveled	to bring to a common level
lied	to speak falsely or utter untruth knowingly
lilted	to sin in a light, tripping or rhythmic manner
lisped	to speak imperfectly
listed	to record item-by-item
loathed	to feel disgust or intense aversion for
lured	to attract, entice or tempt

made clear	to explain fully; to come to light
made known	to bring awareness to
magnified	to increase or make greater
maintained	to keep in an appropriate condition
maligned	to speak harmful untruths about
managed	to bring about; to take charge or care of
manifested	to make clear or evident to the eye or the understanding
marveled	to wonder at
maximized	to increase to the greatest possible amount or degree
mentioned	to refer briefly to
metaphrased	to translate; to change the phrasing
mewled	to cry; whimper
mimicked	to imitate or copy
minimized	to reduce to the smallest possible amount or degree
misled	to lead or guide wrongly
misunderstood	to take in a wrong sense; fail to interpret correctly

mitigated	to lesson in force or intensity; to make less severe
moaned	to utter inarticulately or pitifully
mocked	to ridicule by mimicry; to attack or treat with ridicule, contempt or derision
modulated	to alter or adapt according to the circumstances
mourned	to feel or express sorrow or grief
mouthed	to utter with excessive mouth movements; to form with the lips without actually making an utterance
mouthed off	to talk back
mumbled	to speak in a low indistinct manner, almost to an unintelligible extent
murmured	to speak in a low tone or indistinctly
mused	to think or meditate in silence
muttered	to utter words indistinctly or in a low tone

N

nagged	to annoy persistently
named	to give a name to; to accuse
narrated	to give an account or tell the story
negated	to deny the existence; to nullify
negotiated	to deal or bargain with another
nitpicked	to be criticize by focusing on inconsequential details
nodded	to make a slight, quick downward bending forward of the head
noted	to make particular mention of
notified	to inform or give notice to

objected	to offer a reason or argument in opposition
observed	to regard with attention
offered	to present for acceptance or rejection; to propose
offhanded	to remark without care, thought or consideration
oozed	to exude slowly
opined	to hold or express an opinion
opposed	to act against or provide resistance to
orated	to deliver an oration; to speak pompously
ordered	to direct or command
ousted	to expel or remove from a place
outlined	to give the main features of
owned up	to confess or acknowledge

panicked	to terrify; to become frantic with fear
panted	to breathe hard and quickly
paraphrased	to restate to render the meaning of a phrase
patronized	to behave in an offensively condescending manner toward
peeped	to speak in a thin, weak voice; to utter a short, shrill little cry
perceived	to become aware of, recognize, discern, envision or understand
persisted	to continue steadfastly or firmly; to last or endure tenaciously
persuaded	to prevail up on to do something; to induce to believe by appealing to reason
perused	to browse or read through in a leisurely way
pestered	to bother persistently with petty annoyances
petitioned	to beg for or request; to address a formal petition
philosophized	to speculate or theorize
phonated	to vocalized; to provide a sound source for a given voice or vowel
phrased	to express a word in a particular way

picked	to choose or select; to see and find occasion for; provoke
piped up	to make oneself heard; speak up; to assert oneself
pitched	to set in a fixed position; to suggest
played dumb	to pretend to be slow-witted or lacking specific knowledge
pleaded	to appeal or entreat earnestly
pledged	to promise solemnly
pointed	to indicate the presence or position of
pointed out	to call attention to
pondered	to consider something deeply and thoroughly
popped off	to make a short, quick explosive sound
portended	to indicate in advance; to foreshadow
posed	to assert, state or put forward
postulated	to ask, demand or claim
pouted	to thrust out the lips; to look or be sullen
praised	to express approval or admiration of; to offer grateful homage to
prattled	to talk in a foolish or simple-minded way
prayed	to offer devout petition, praise, thanks; to make entreaty or supplication
preached	to proclaim or make known by sermon
predicated	to proclaim; declare; affirm
predicted	to declare or tell in advance
premised	to set forth beforehand

presaged	to portend, foreshadow
presented	to introduce to the public
pressed	to act exert force or pressure
presumed	to take for granted, assume or suppose
pretended	to appear falsely; feign
prevaricated	to speak falsely or misleadingly
pried	to inquire impertinently or unnecessarily into something
probed	to search into or examine thoroughly
proceeded	to move or go forward; to emerge or originate
proclaimed	to announce or declare in an official or open way
prodded	to rouse or incite; nag
profaned	to treat with irreverence or contempt
professed	to declare openly; to lay claim to; announce or affirm
proffered	to put before a person for acceptance
promised	to declare that something will or will not be done; to express assurance on which expectation
prognosticated	to forecast or predict from present indications or signs
promoted	to help or encourage to exist
prompted	to move or induce; incite
promulgated	to make known by open declaration
pronounced	to enunciate or articulate; to utter or sound in a particular manner in speaking

prophesied	to foretell or predict
proposed	to offer or suggest for consideration
propounded	to put forward or offer for consideration, acceptance or adoption
protested	to give manifest expression to objection or disapproval
proved	to establish the truth or genuineness of
publicized	to bring to public notice
purported	to present the appearance of being; profess or claim falsely
purred	to utter a low, continuous, murmuring sound expressive of contentment or pleasure
pursued	to follow close upon
pushed	to press upon, often with force
put in	to bring to relation

quacked	to utter the cry of a duck or a sound resembling it
quaked	to shake or tremble
qualified	to modify or limit in some way; to provide with proper knowledge
quarreled	to disagree angrily
quavered	to sound, speak or sing tremulously
queried	to ask or inquire about
questioned	to ask or inquire about
quibbled	to equivocate; to carp
quipped	to utter a clever or witty remark or comment
quizzed	to examine or test
quoted	to repeat words from a passage or phrase

rang out	to give forth a clear resonant sound
raged	to act or speak with fury
railed	to utter bitter complaint or vehement denunciation
rambled	to speak with a lack of organization
ranted	to speak or declaim extravagantly or violently; talk in a wild or vehement way
rapped	to utter sharply or vigorously
rasped	to make a grating sound
ratified	to confirm by expressing consent
rationalized	to remove unreasonable elements from; to ascribe to causes that superficially seem reasonable and valid but that actually are unrelated to the true causes
rattled off	to talk rapidly and at length, often a list
raved	to talk wildly; to talk with extravagant enthusiasm
reacted	to act in response
read	to utter aloud or render in speech written or printed words
reaffirmed	to state or assert positively; to confirm or ratify

reawakened	to awaken again; to spring into being, arise, originate
reasoned	to think or argue in a logical manner
reassured	to restore to assurance or confidence
rebuffed	to give a blunt or abrupt rejection
rebuked	to express shark, stern disapproval of
rebutted	to refute by evidence or argument
recalled	to bring back from memory; recollect
recanted	to withdraw or disavow
reciprocated	to give, feel, in return
recited	to repeat the words of from memory
reckoned	to esteem or consider
recollected	to recall to mind
recommended	to represent or urge as advisable or expedient
reconciled	to win over to friendliness; cause to become amicable
recorded	to cause to be set down or registered
recounted	to relate or narrate
recovered	to cover again or anew
recriminated	to bring a countercharge against an accuser
rectified	to make, put or set right
reeled off	to talk rapidly and at length, often a list
referred	to direct for information or anything required; to direct the attention or thoughts of
reflected	to give back to; to think seriously

refused	to decline to accept or give
refuted	to prove to be false or erroneous
regarded	to look upon or think of; to have or show respect; to pay attention
registered	to express with the face and body; to realize and acknowledge internally
regretted	to feel sorrow or remorse for
regurgitated	to give back or repeat
rehearsed	to practice
reiterated	to say or do again or repeatedly
rejected	to refuse to have, take, recognize or grant
rejoiced	to be glad; take delight
rejoined	to come again into the company of; reunite
related	to tell; give an account of
released	to free from anything that restrains
remained	to continue in the same state; to stay behind or in the same place
remarked	to say casually; to note
remembered	to recall to the mind
reminded	to cause to remember
reminisced	to recall past experiences
remonstrated	to say or plead in protest or objection or disapproval
rendered	to cause to be or become
renounced	to give up or put aside voluntarily

remunerated	to mention separately; specify, as in a list; to ascertain the number of
repeated	to say or utter again
replied	to make answer; to respond
reported	to carry and repeat as an answer or message; to relate
reprehended	to reprove or find fault with
represented	to serve to express, designate, stand for or denote
reprimanded	to reprove or rebuke severely
reproved	to criticize or correct; to disapprove of strongly
reputed	to consider or believe to be as specified
requested	to ask or beg for
resolved	to come to a definite or earnest decision about
responded	to reply
restated	to state again or in a new way
restored	to bring back to a former, original or normal condition
resumed	to take up or go on with again
retaliated	to return like for like
retorted	to reply to in a sharp or retaliatory way
retreated	to withdraw, retire or draw back
returned	to revert; to give back in reciprocation
revealed	to make known
reveled	to take great pleasure or delight

reworded	to put into other words
rhapsodize	to talk with extravagant enthusiasm
ridiculed	to deride; make fun of
righted	to put in proper order, condition, or relationship
risked	to venture upon
roared	to utter a loud, deep cry or howl
rumbled	to make a deep, heavy, somewhat muffled, continuous sound
ruminated	to meditate or muse
rushed	to convey with haste

sanctioned	to authorize, approve or allow; to ratify or confirm
sang	to utter words or sounds in succession with musical modulations of the voice
sang out	to call in a loud voice
sassed	to answer back in an impudent manner
schemed	to devise a plan or plot
scoffed	to speak derisively
scolded	to find fault with angrily
scorned	to treat or regard with contempt
screamed	to utter a loud, sharp, piercing cry
screeched	to utter or make a harsh, shrill cry or sound
scrutinized	to examine in detail with careful or critical attention
second-guessed	to use hindsight in criticizing or correcting
seconded	to assist or support
seethed	to be in a state of agitation or excitement
sermonized	to give exhortation to

settled	to agree upon; to resolve definitely and conclusively
shamed	to cause to feel disgraced
shared	to give part
shifted	to manage to get along or succeed by oneself
shot back	to reply quickly
shouted	to call or cry out loudly and vigorously
shrieked	a loud, sharp, shrill cry
shrilled	to emit a sharp high-pitched sound
shrugged	to express indifference, disdain
shuddered	to tremble with a sudden convulsive movement
shunned	to keep away from; take pains to avoid
sighed	to let out one's breath audibly; to yearn or long
simplified	to make less complex or complicated
singled out	to point out or show prejudice against
singsonged	to express in monotonous rhythmical cadence
sizzled	to express heatedly
slid in	to inject or interrupt
slurred	to pronounce indistinctly; to pass over lightly or without due mention
smacked	to strike sharply; to smack the lips

smarted off	to answer back in an impudent manner
smiled	to assume or give a smile; to express by a smile
smoldered	to exist or continue in a suppressed state; undergo slow or suppressed combustion
snapped	to say suddenly and sharply
snarled	to speak in a surly or threatening manner
sneered	to contort the face in a manner that shows scorn or contempt; to speak in a manner expressive of derision
snickered	to laugh in a half=suppressed, indecorous or disrespectful manner
snipped	to say sharply and quickly
snitched	to turn informer
sniveled	to weep or cry with sniffling
snooped	to prowl or pry
snorted	to express contempt, indignation; to force the breath violently through the nostrils with a loud, harsh sound
sobbed	to weep with a convulsive catching of the breath
solicited	to entreat or petition
soliloquized	to read out loud; to narrate to oneself
soothed	to tranquilize or cam; relieve; comfort
sought	to try to find or discovered by searching or questioning

sounded	to make or emit a sound; to give forth a sound as a call or summons
sounded off	to call out one's name; to speak freely or frankly; to exaggerate or boast
spared	to deal gently or leniently with; to release or relieve
spat	to engage in a petty quarrel or dispute; to express hatred or contempt
specified	to state in detail
speculated	to engage in thought or reflection; to indulge in conjectural thought
speed-talked	to talk quickly
spelled	to express words by letters
spelled out	to explain something explicitly
spewed	to flow out or issue suddenly; to express oneself extravagantly or emotionally
spilled	to utter or confess something
spoke	to utter words or articulate sounds with the ordinary voice
spouted	to state or declaim volubly or in an oratorical manner
sprayed	to speak with such enunciation that spittle leave the mouth
spread	to extend or cause to extend over a large expanse
spurted	to state or declaim volubly or in an oratorical manner
sputtered	incoherent stammering speech
squawked	to complain loudly and vehemently
squeaked	to utter or sound with a short, sharp, shrill cry

squealed	to confess or turn informer
stalled	to delay or put off, especially by evasion or deception
stammered	to speak with involuntary breaks and pauses, or with spasmodic repetitions of syllables or sounds
started	to begin
stated	to declare definitely or specifically
stipulated	to make an express demand or arrangement as a condition of agreement
stood	to face or encounter
stormed	to rage or complain with violence or fury
strained	to exert to the utmost
stressed	to emphasize
strived	to exert oneself vigorously
studied	to examine or investigate carefully; to apply oneself to acquiring knowledge
struggled	to exert strength, energy and force
stuttered	to speak with recurring repetition of consonants
submitted	to give over or yield to the power or authority of another
subscribed	to pledge to give or pay money as a contribution, gift or investment
suggested	to mention or introduce for consideration or possible action
summoned	to call upon

supported	to bear or hold up; to serve as a foundation for
supposed	to assume; to consider as a possibility suggested
surmised	to think or infer without certain or strong evidence
surrendered	to yield to the possession of power or power of another
swore	to bind oneself by oath; to use profanity
symbolized	to stand for or represent in the manner of a symbol
sympathized	to fell or express compassion; to share or understand the sentiments or ideas

talked	to communicate or exchange ideas
tantalized	to torment with; tease by arousing expectations
tattled	to let out secrets; to chatter, prate or gossip
taunted	to reproach in a sarcastic, insulting or jeering manner
teased	to irritate or provoke with persistent petty distractions
tempted	to entice or allure; to attract or appeal strongly to
termed	to apply a particular term or name to
testified	to bear witness; to give evidence
thanked	to express gratitude, appreciation or acknowledgment
theorized	to form a theory
thought	to employ one's mind rationally and objectively in evaluating or dealing with a given situation
thought aloud	to speak out loud what has formed in the mind
threatened	to indicate impending evil or mischief
thrust	to put boldly forth or impose acceptance of
thundered	to strike, give forth with loud noise or violent action

ticked off	to mark with ticks; checked in order
tipped off	to supply private or secret information; to warn of impending danger or trouble
tisked	to make a tisk sound; to express concern or approval
told	to give an account or narrative to
tolerated	to endure without repugnance
tooted	to give or cause to give a short blast, hoot or whistle
touted	to solicit support for importunately; to describe or advertise boastfully
trailed off	to slowly fade
transferred	to cause to pass from one person to another
transmitted	to communicate; to send or forward
translated	to change the form
tried	to attempt to do or accomplish
trilled	to utter or make a sound or succession of sounds resembling a vibratory or quavering effect
trumpeted	to emit a loud cry
twanged	to give out a sharp, vibrating sound; a nasal vocal sound
tweeted	to make a weak chirping sound; to post a message on Twitter
twittered	to talk lightly and rapidly

ululated	to howl, to wail, to lament shrilly, without words
uncovered	to lay bare; disclose
underestimated	to think insufficiently highly of
unleashed	to abandon control of
unveiled	to reveal or disclose
upbraided	to find fault with or reproach severely
urged	to make entreaties or earnest recommendations
uttered	to give audible expression to

validated	to substantiate; confirm
vaunted	to praise boastfully or excessively
vented	to give free play or expression to; to give public utterance to
ventilated	to give utterance or expression to one's emotions, opinions, complaints
ventriloquized	to speak or sound in the manner of a ventriloquist
ventured	to take the risk of
verbalized	to express in words
verified	to prove the truth of; to ascertain the truth or correctness of
vetoed	to reject; to prohibit emphatically
vindicated	to clear from an accusation or suspicion, to afford justification for
vocalized	to endow with a voice
vociferated	to speak or cry out loudly or noisily
voiced	to give utterance or expression to
volunteered	to give, bestow or performed voluntarily
vouched	to support as being true, certain or reliable
vowed	to pledge or resolve solemnly to do

waffled	to speak equivocally about
wailed	to utter a prolonged, inarticulate, mournful cry, usually high-pitched
wangled	to falsify or manipulate for dishonest ends
wanted to know	to derive knowledge from asking; being curious
warbled	to sing or whistle with trills, quavers or melodic embellishments
warned	to urge or advise to be careful; caution
warranted	to give authority to
watered down	to make weaker or less effective
wavered	to be irresolute; hesitant between two possibilities; to become unsteady
weighed	to hold up or balance
went along	to go with; follow
went on	to proceed
wept	to express grief, sorrow or any overpowering emotion by shedding tears
wheedled	to persuade; to endeavor to influence by smooth, flattering or beguiling words
wheezed	to breathe with difficulty and with a whistling sound

whimpered	to cry with low, plaintive, broken sounds
whined	to utter a low, complaining cry or sound; to snivel or complain in a peevish self-pitying way
whispered	to speak with soft hushed sounds
whistled	to produce shrill or flutelike sounds
whooped	to utter a loud cry or shout in expressing enthusiasm, excitement
wiled	to beguile, entice or lure
winked	to close and open one eye quickly, deliberately or in an exaggerated fashion to convey friendliness
wisecracked	to make smart or facetious remarks
wished	to want, desire or long for
wondered	to think or speculate curiously; to be filled with admiration, amazement or awe
worded	to express in words
wore on	to continue in a durable fashion; droned
worried	to torment oneself with or suffer from disturbing thoughts; fret; to move with effort

NONE

yakked	to talk uninterruptedly and idly
yammered	to whine or complain; to make an outcry or clamor
yapped	to bark sharply, shrilly or snappishly
yawned	to say with a yawn; to open wide like a mouth
yawped	to utter a loud, harsh cry; to yelp; to talk noisily and foolishly
yearned	to have an earnest or strong desire; to feel tenderness
yelled	to cry out or speak with a strong, loud, clear sound
yelped	to give a quick, sharp, shrill cry; to call or cry out sharply
yielded	to produce or furnish; to surrender or submit
yodeled	to sing with frequent changes from the ordinary voice to falsetto and back again; to call or shout in a similar fashion
yowled	to utter a long, distressful or dismal cry

zapped	to attack, defeat or destroy with sudden speed or force
zig-zagged	to escape from by trickery or cleverness, usually switching topics immediately
zipped through	to complete quickly

Get my FREE E-Report!

<u>6 Secrets of Successful Writers</u>

Don't wait! <u>Get it now!</u>

Do you want to be a successful writer?

My guide *6 Assets Every Writer Needs To Be Successful* will give you a helpful insight to what it is you need to have in your arsenal to give you a start on your road to being successful.

It's nearly impossible to be a successful writer without these six things. Do you know what they are? If you don't or only think you do this guide is perfect for you.

And because I want to help you achieve your dreams I will give you this writing guide for free. Just click the link below and enter your name and email and this wonderful resource will be yours!

Yes! I would like to know the <u>6 Secrets Of Successful Writers</u>

Available at:

www.midnighttaylor.com/free-writing-guide

Also Available:

550 Ways To Say Went

abandoned absquatulated barnstormed beelined careened cir
cumambulated dawdled departed embarked escaped flounced
forged galumphed glissaded hastened hurdled impelled inch
d jogged junketed la   unched limped ma
ndered migrated   neared paced
erambulated q   uivered ran
ed relocated   sallied for
th scramble   d tiptoed
traipsed va   ulted vo
aged wadd   led waf
led zoomed   abandon
d absquatul   ated barn
stormed beel   ined care

550 Ways To Say Went

Midnight Taylor

med circumam A "Writing By Midnight" Resource bulated da
dled departed em   barked escap
d flounced forged g   alumphed glissa
ed hastened hurdled im   pelled inched jogged j
nketed launched limpe   d maundered migrated neared
aced perambulated qu   ivered ranged relocated sallied fo
th scrambled tiptoed   traipsed vaulted voyaged waddled w
ffled zoomed abandoned absquatulated barnstormed beeline
careened circumambulated dawdled departed embarked esc
ped flounced forged galumphed glissaded hastened hurdle
impelled inched jogged junketed launched limped maundere
migrated neared paced perambulated quivered ranged reloc

About Midnight

Midnight Taylor has been writing since the age of 13. Starting out with short stories and poems and graduating to owning her website and publishing non-fiction works and novels.

Midnight's resource books are made in an effort to provide valuable information and resources to aspiring writers as well as those who have already accomplished achievements in the craft. These books are also a great tool for students and those wishing to further their knowledge.

Midnight's true passion is her poetry and fiction writing. Her poetry has started to be published in volumes titled "Shadows of Myself" and her novel series is also available.

You can find her other works at www.midnighttaylor.com.

Celebrate. Advance. Dream. Enjoy. Love.